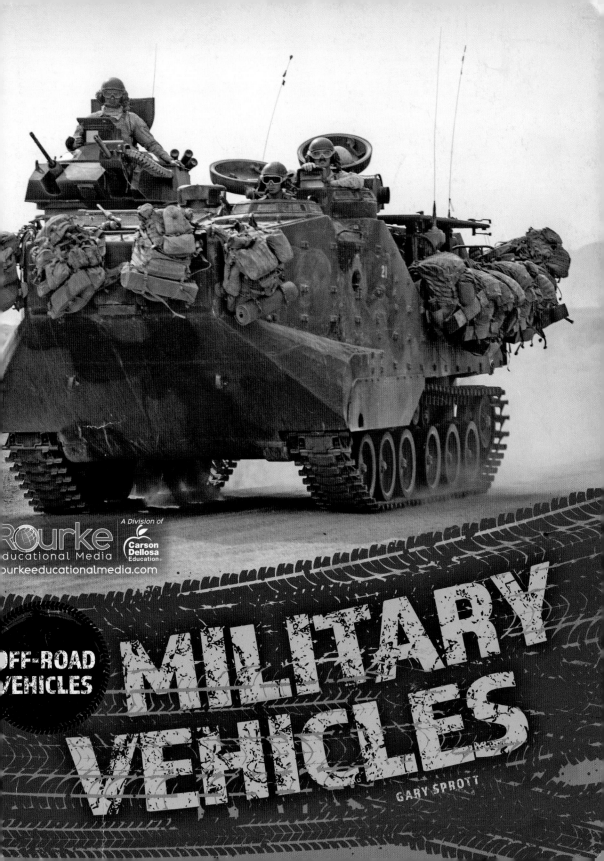

Rourke
Educational Media
ourkeeducationalmedia.com

A Division of
Carson
Dellosa
Education

OFF-ROAD
VEHICLES

MILITARY VEHICLES

GARY SPROTT

Before Reading: *Building Background Knowledge and Vocabulary*

Building background knowledge can help children process new information and build upon what they already know. Before reading a book, it is important to tap into what children already know about the topic. This will help them develop their vocabulary and increase their reading comprehension.

Questions and Activities to Build Background Knowledge:

1. Look at the front cover of the book and read the title. What do you think this book will be about?
2. What do you already know about this topic?
3. Take a book walk and skim the pages. Look at the table of contents, photographs, captions, and bold words. Did these text features give you any information or predictions about what you will read in this book?

Vocabulary: *Vocabulary Is Key to Reading Comprehension*

Use the following directions to prompt a conversation about each word.

- Read the vocabulary words.
- What comes to mind when you see each word?
- What do you think each word means?

Vocabulary Words:
- assault
- civilian
- horsepower
- obstacles
- prototype
- surveillance
- vital

During Reading: *Reading for Meaning and Understanding*

To achieve deep comprehension of a book, children are encouraged to use close reading strategies. During reading, it is important to have children stop and make connections. These connections result in deeper analysis and understanding of a book.

 Close Reading a Text

During reading, have children stop and talk about the following:

- Any confusing parts
- Any unknown words
- Text to text, text to self, text to world connections
- The main idea in each chapter or heading

Encourage children to use context clues to determine the meaning of any unknown words. These strategies will help children learn to analyze the text more thoroughly as they read.

When you are finished reading this book, turn to the next-to-last **page for**
After Reading Questions and an **Activity**.

TABLE OF CONTENTS

Trusty Tanks 4

By Land and Sea.......................................14

Keeping Them Safe................................20

Memory Game..30

Index 31

After Reading Questions......................31

Activity...31

About the Author 32

TRUSTY TANKS

Armies have been using motorized vehicles for more than 100 years. Amazing inventions travel on land and through water. Tanks rumble into battle. Armored carriers transport troops to safety.

The first tank was made in England in 1915 during World War I. It was called Little Willie, but it was a beast! The **prototype** of the tank was so heavy, it got stuck in the mud.

prototype (PROH-tuh-tipe): the first version of an invention that tests an idea to see if it will work

A tank can weigh more than a humpback whale! But these monstrous machines have tremendous **horsepower** and can travel at highway speeds.

horsepower (HORS-pou-ur): a unit for measuring the power of an engine; based on the work ability of a horse

Making Tracks!

Tanks have tracks, or treads, over their wheels so they can handle the toughest terrain. The tracks move like a conveyor belt in a grocery store checkout lane.

The M1 Abrams is the United States Army's main fighting tank. With its cannon and machine guns, the tank has mighty firepower. It uses a laser to find its target and can hit objects more than two miles (3.2 kilometers) away.

Spinning Top

Four soldiers can travel inside the M1 Abrams. They are protected by its heavy armor. The top of the tank, known as the turret, can spin all the way around like a merry-go-round.

Military vehicles are built to operate in many environments. Battles are fought in deserts, cities, mountains, forests, and open ranges. Vehicles must be able to withstand extreme heat, heights, tight spaces, and more.

Mighty Mutt!

The Multi-Utility Tactical Transport, or MUTT, looks like a tiny tank. This robotic vehicle is armed with a machine gun and carries cargo to support troops.

Military vehicles can maneuver through narrow city streets.

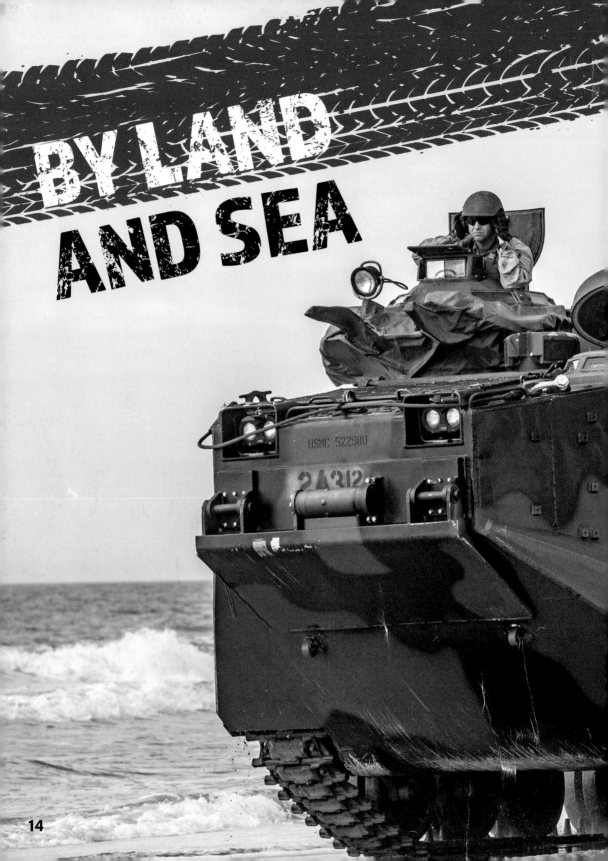

BY LAND AND SEA

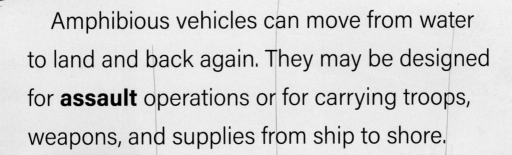

Amphibious vehicles can move from water to land and back again. They may be designed for **assault** operations or for carrying troops, weapons, and supplies from ship to shore.

Gator to the Rescue!

The first amphibious assault vehicles were built in the 1930s. They were based on the Alligator, a vehicle designed to rescue hurricane victims in Florida.

assault (uh-SAWLT): attack

The Viking is an all-terrain, amphibious vehicle used by the British Royal Marines. It can move through mud, sand, and snow. It can cross rivers, lakes, and other **obstacles**. If attacked, the armored Viking can defend itself with machine guns and smoke grenades.

obstacles (AHB-stuh-kuhlz): things that get in the way or prevent something from moving forward

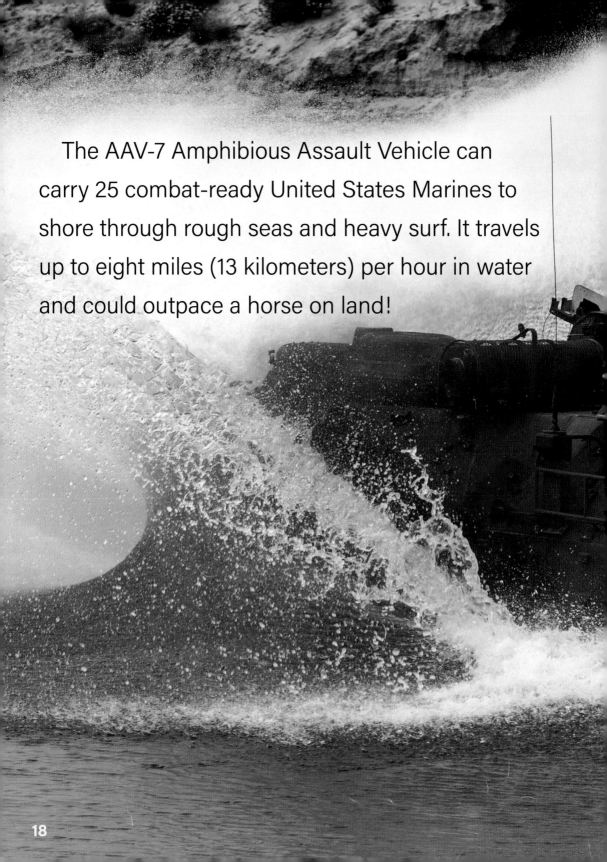

The AAV-7 Amphibious Assault Vehicle can carry 25 combat-ready United States Marines to shore through rough seas and heavy surf. It travels up to eight miles (13 kilometers) per hour in water and could outpace a horse on land!

Legendary Warriors

Amphibious vehicles helped turn
the tide of World War II. The
Allied nations, including the
United States and Britain, landed
tens of thousands of troops on the
beaches of Europe and the Pacific
in surprise attacks.

KEEPING THEM SAFE

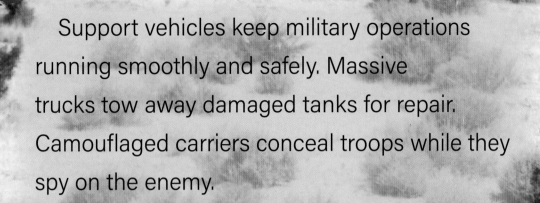

Support vehicles keep military operations running smoothly and safely. Massive trucks tow away damaged tanks for repair. Camouflaged carriers conceal troops while they spy on the enemy.

Clearing the Path

The U.S. Army's six-wheeled Buffalo has a long mechanical arm to clear land mines and other dangerous devices. The vehicle's heavy armor helps protect it from explosive blasts.

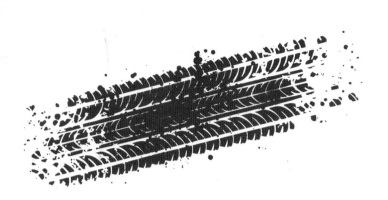

It has a fancy name but a simple mission. The Palletized Load System (PLS) A1 hauls 20-foot (six-meter) long cargo containers with **vital** supplies for advancing troops. This ten-wheeled giant has a driver's cab shaped like a bulldog's face—it's truly a soldier's best friend!

vital (VYE-tuhl): very important or essential

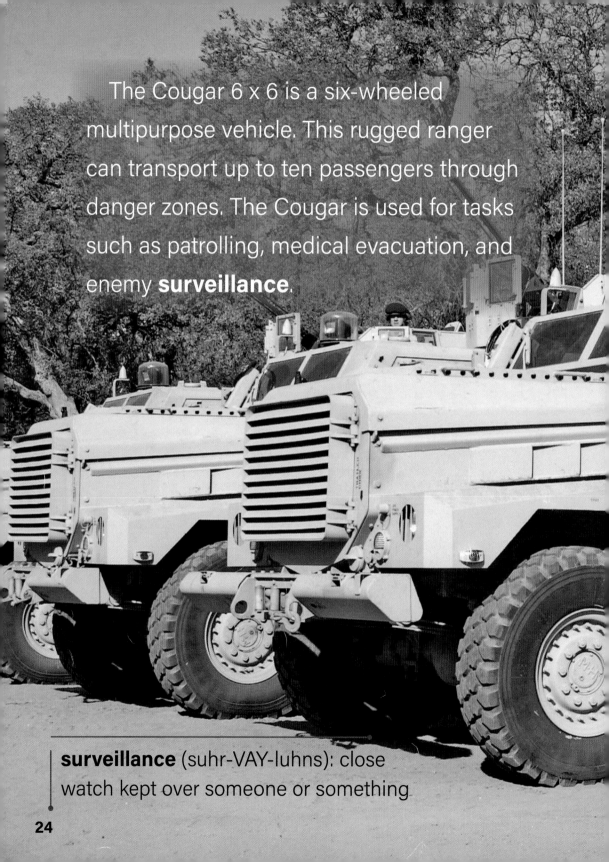

The Cougar 6 x 6 is a six-wheeled multipurpose vehicle. This rugged ranger can transport up to ten passengers through danger zones. The Cougar is used for tasks such as patrolling, medical evacuation, and enemy **surveillance**.

surveillance (suhr-VAY-luhns): close watch kept over someone or something

Military Muscle

The Cougar belongs to a category of military vehicles known as Mine-Resistant Ambush Protected (MRAP). Its hardened exterior is designed to withstand armor-piercing bullets, rocket-launched grenades, and land mines.

The Bradley Fighting Vehicle is a tank-like troop transport. The armor-shielded Bradley is equipped with a cannon and machine gun to defend against enemy tanks and helicopters.

Obstacle Course Champ

The Bradley Fighting Vehicle is built for mobility. It can cross an eight-foot (2.4-meter) trench and scale a three-foot (one-meter) wall!

You don't have to be in the military to drive a military vehicle! Jeeps and Hummers began life in the armed forces before they were converted into **civilian** vehicles. Now, you might see them transporting toddlers instead of troops!

civilian (suh-VIL-yuhn): not related to the military

Memory Game

Look at the pictures. What do you remember
reading on the pages where each image appeared?

Index

amphibious 15, 16, 18, 19

armor(ed) 4, 11, 16, 21, 25, 26

Bradley Fighting Vehicle 26, 27

cargo 12, 22

Hummers 28

land mines 21, 25

surveillance 24

weapons 15

After Reading Questions

1. What was the name of the first tank?

2. Why do tanks have tracks?

3. When were the first amphibious assault vehicles built?

4. What do passenger vehicles such as Jeeps and Hummers have in common?

5. How fast can the AAV-7 Amphibious Assault Vehicle travel in water?

Activity

Do you know someone who is serving or who has served in the military? Write ten questions to ask this person about the types of vehicles they used while in the armed forces. With an adult's permission, ask this person if you can interview them. Write a news article or fictional story based on their answers.

About the Author

Gary Sprott is a writer in Tampa, Florida. He has written books about ancient cultures, animals, plants, and automobiles. Gary wishes he had an amphibious vehicle because his car was once flooded in a hurricane.

www.rourkeeducationalmedia.com

PHOTO CREDITS: Cover and Title Page ©Lance Cpl. Levi Schultz; Pg 5, 30 ©Cpl. Joseph Prado; Pg 14, 30 ©Lance Cpl. Immanuel Johnson; Pg 23, 30 ©Oshkosh Defense ; Pg 20, 30 ©Ken Drylie, Civ, USA; Pg 29, 30 ©contrastaddict; Pg 9, 30 ©Cpl. Gabrielle Quire; Pg 7 ©Library of Congress; Pg 10 ©Cpl. Gabrielle Quire; Pg 13 ©Staff Sgt Aaron Allmon; Pg 17 ©PO(Phot) Dave Gallagher; Pg 18 ©Lance Cpl. Drake Nickels; Pg 24 ©MC2 Dustin Coveny, USN; Pg 26 ©SSgt Shane A. Cuomo

Edited by: Kim Thompson
Cover and interior design by: Rhea Magaro-Wallace

Library of Congress PCN Data

Military Vehicles / Gary Sprott
(Off-Road Vehicles)
ISBN 978-1-73161-455-1 (hard cover)
ISBN 978-1-73161-256-4 (soft cover)
ISBN 978-1-73161-560-2 (e-Book)
ISBN 978-1-73161-665-4 (ePub)
Library of Congress Control Number: 2019932457

Rourke Educational Media
Printed in the United States of America,
North Mankato, Minnesota